POEMS THAT HAVE HELPED ME

POEMS THAT HAVE HELPED ME

EDITED BY S.E. KISER

LAUGHING ELEPHANT BOOKS   SEATTLE   2000

POEMS THAT HAVE HELPED ME

A reprint of a book originally published
by P.F. Volland and Company in 1913.

ISBN 1-883211-26-3

Laughing Elephant Books
Post Office Box 4399   Seattle Washington   98104

MONG the things that you like to treasure there are two or three or perhaps a half dozen poems. Possibly they are poems you "learned by heart" when you went to school, or it may be that you have found them among the "fugitive verses" which are printed from time to time in newspapers or religious publications.

It may be that you never have acknowledged even to yourself how much these poems, whether they are tucked away in your memory or in your pocketbook, have helped you. Nevertheless, they have served you in no small degree. They have encouraged you when you needed encouragement; they have been a solace to you in those moments when you felt the need of something to strengthen your faith or rekindle your hope.

The poems contained in this collection have in most cases found favor with other compilers. With a few exceptions they have long been doing duty as "old favorites," to be found here and there in scrap books or buried within the depths of bulky volumes such as collectors generally deem it necessary to put forth. It is for the purpose of placing these masterpieces of the poets within easy reach of those who occasionally feel the need of encouragement and consolation that the present compilation is offered.

There are people, no doubt, who have never, after reading an inspiring poem, risen with renewed determination and strengthened hopes—who have never, after suffering defeat or bereavement, found in some well remembered line or stanza a comforting word or a message of cheer. To these unfortunate ones this little book will make no appeal but to the many who have been made better and stronger and nobler and kinder because their hearts have responded to the appeal of the inspired poet—because they have lacked only the power of expression to be worthy of enrollment among the immortals—this symposium is dedicated.

An effort has been made to keep the volume small, to avoid the inclusion of poems that might have a tendency to defeat or obscure the purpose for which the collection was intended. In some cases but one or two stanzas have been taken from long poems. It is not necessary to read a lengthy sermon from Burns when he can give us in the two lines,

"O, wad some power the giftie gie us
To see oursels as ithers see us."
all the philosophy we need to make us charitable.

The present compiler is not ashamed to say that his patriotic impulses have been stirred, that he has been comforted in affliction, that he has been strengthened in adversity, that he has been lured from the mazes of doubt, by these poems. It is with the hope that they may serve others as they have served him that they are now presented.

—S. E. K.

CONCORD HYMN

BY the rude bridge that arched the flood,
  Their flag to April's breeze unfurled,
Here once the embattled farmers stood,
  And fired the shot heard round the world.

The foe long since in silence slept;
  Alike the conqueror silent sleeps;
And Time the ruined bridge has swept
  Down the dark stream which seaward creeps.

On the green bank, by this soft stream,
  We set today a votive stone;
That memory may their deed redeem,
  When, like our sires, our sons are gone.

Spirit, that made those heroes dare
  To die, or leave their children free,
Bid Time and Nature gently spare
  The shaft we raise to them and thee.

—Ralph Waldo Emerson

SONG

GIVE me back my heart, fair child;
    To you as yet 'twere worth but little;
Half beguiler, half beguiled,
    Be you warned, your own is brittle,
I know it by your redd'ning cheeks,
I know it by those two black streaks
Arching up your pearly brows
    In a momentary laughter,
Stretched in long and dark repose
    With a sigh the moment after.

"Hid it; dropt it on the moors!
    Lost it, and you can not find it"—
My own heart I want, not yours
    You have bound and must unbind it.
Set it free then from your net,
We will love, sweet—but not yet!
Fling it from you—we are strong
    Love is trouble, love is folly;
Love, that makes an old heart young,
    Makes a young heart melancholy.

—Aubrey de Vere

SO here has been dawning
    Another blue day;
Think, will thou let it
    Slip useless away?

—Carlyle

ACTION

COME, fill the cup, and in the fire of Spring
    Your Winter garment of repentance fling;
The bird of Time has but a little way
    To flutter—and the bird is on the wing.

—Omar Khayyam

FAITH

WE have but faith; we cannot know;
    For knowledge is of things we see;
    And yet we trust it comes from thee,
A beam of darkness: let it grow.

Let knowledge grow from more to more,
    But more of reverence in us dwell;
    That mind and soul, according well,
May make one music as before,

But vaster. We are fools and slight;
    We mock thee when we do not fear;
    But help thy foolish ones to bear;
Help thy vain worlds to bear thy light.

Forgive what seemed my sin in me;
    What seem'd my worth since I began;
    For merit lies from man to man,
And not from man, O Lord, to thee.

—Tennyson

From "In Memoriam"

THE FOOL'S PRAYER

THE royal feast was done; the king
    Sought some new sport to banish care,
And to his jester cried: "Sir Fool,
    Kneel now, and make for us a prayer."

The jester doffed his cap and bells
    And stood the mocking court before;
They could not see the bitter smile
    Behind the painted grin he wore.

He bowed his head and bent his knee
    Upon the monarch's silken stool;
His pleading voice arose: "O Lord,
    Be merciful to me, a fool!

"No pity, Lord, could change the heart
    From red with wrong to white as wool;
The rod must heal the sin; but, Lord,
    Be merciful to me, a fool!

"'Tis not by guilt the onward sweep
    Of truth and right, O Lord, we stay!
'Tis by our follies that so long
    We hold the earth from heaven away.

"These clumsy feet, still in the mire,
    Go crushing blossoms without end;
These hard, well-meaning hands we thrust
    Among the heart-strings of a friend.

"The ill-timed truth we might have kept—
    Who knows how sharp it pierced and stung!
The word we had not sense to say—
    Who knows how grandly it had rung!

"Our faults no tenderness should ask,
    The clustering stripes must cleanse them all;
But for our blunders—oh, in shame
    Before the eyes of heaven we fall.

"Earth bears no balsams for mistakes;
    Men crown the knave and scourge the tool
That did his will; but, Thou, O Lord,
    Be merciful to me, a fool!"

The room was hushed; in silence rose
    The king, and sought his gardens cool,
And walked apart, and murmured low,
    "Be merciful to me, a fool!"

—Edward Rowland Sill

VICE

VICE is a monster of such hideous mien
    That to be hated needs but to be seen;
Yet seen too oft, familiar with her face,
We first endure, then pity, then embrace.

—Alexander Pope

TIMES GO BY TURNS

THE lopped tree in time may grow again,
  Most naked plants renew both fruit and flower;
The sorriest wight may find release of pain,
  The driest soil suck in some moistening shower;
Time goes by turns, and chances change by course,
  From foul to fair, from better hap to worse.

The sea of Fortune doth not ever flow;
  She draws her favors to the lowest ebb;
Her tides have equal times to come and go;
  Her loom doth weave the fine and coarsest web;
No joy so great but runneth to an end,
  No hap so hard but may in fine amend.

Not always fall of leaf, nor ever Spring;
  Not endless night, yet not eternal day;
The saddest birds a season find to sing;
  The roughest storm a calm may soon allay.
Thus, with succeeding turns God tempereth all,
  That man may hope to rise, yet fear to fall.

A chance may win that by mischance was lost;
  That net that holds no great takes little fish;
In some things all, in all things none are crost;
  Few all they need, but none have all they wish.
Unmingled joys here to no man befall;
  Who least, hath some; who most, hath never all.

—Robert Southwell

THE BRAVE AT HOME

THE maid who binds her warrior's sash
    With smile that all her pain dissembles,
The while beneath her drooping lash
    One starry tear-drop hangs and trembles,
Though heaven alone records the tear,
    And Fame shall never know her story,
Her heart has shed a drop as dear
    As e'er bedewed the field of glory.

The wife who girds her husband's sword,
    'Mid little ones who weep or wonder,
And bravely speaks the cheering word,
    What though her heart be rent asunder,
Doomed nightly in her dreams to hear
    The bolts of death around him rattle,
Has shed as sacred blood as e'er
    Was poured upon the field of battle.

The mother who conceals her grief
    While to her breast her son she presses,
Then breathes a few brave words and brief,
    Kissing the patriot brow she blesses,
With no one but her secret God
    To know the pain that weighs upon her,
Sheds holy blood as e'er the sod
    Received on Freedom's field of honor.

                                        —Thomas Buchanan Read

LAUGH LITTLE FELLOW

LAUGH, little fellow, laugh and sing
And just be glad for everything!
Be glad for morning and for night,
For sun and stars that laugh with light,
For trees that chuckle in the breeze,
For singing birds and humming bees—
Be one with them, and laugh along
And weave their gladness in your song.

Let nothing but the twinkle-tears
Come to your eyes these happy years,
When you are free of task and toil
And all the frets that come to spoil
The hours of folk whose feet have paced
The road along which all must haste—
Laugh, little fellow, for it drives
The shadows out of other lives.

Go romping care-free as you will
Across the meadow, up the hill,
And shout your message far away
For all the world to join your play.
This is the time for laughter: now,
When Time has not set on your brow
The finger-prints that come with care
And leave abiding wrinkles there.

Laugh, little fellow, laugh and sing
And coax the joy from everything;
Take gladness at its fullest worth
And make each hour an hour of mirth,
So that when on the downward slope
Of life the radiant sky of hope
Will bend above you all the way
And make you happy, as today.

—Wilbur D. Nesbit

FRIENDS

FRIEND after friend departs;
   Who hath not lost a friend?
There is no union here of hearts
   That finds not here an end;
Were this frail world our only rest,
   Living or dying, none were blest.

Beyond the flight of Time,
   Beyond this vale of death,
There surely is some blessed clime
   Where life is not a breath,
Nor life's affections transient fire
   Whose sparks fly upward to expire.

—James Montgomety

WARREN'S ADDRESS

 TAND! the ground's your own, my braves!
Will ye give it up to slaves?
Will ye look for greener graves?
    Hope ye mercy still?
What's the mercy despots feel?
Hear it in that battle peal!
Read it on yon bristling steel!
    Ask it—ye who will!

Fear ye foes who kill for hire?
Will ye to your homes retire?
Look behind you! they're afire!
    And, before you, see
Who have done it! From the vale
On they come! and will ye quail?
Leaden rain and iron hail
    Let their welcome be!

In the God of battles trust!
Die we may—and die we must;
But, O, where can dust to dust
    Be consigned so well
As where heaven its dews shall shed
On the martyred patriot's bed,
And the rocks shall raise their head
    Of his deeds to tell.

—John Pierpont

ONWARD

WE are living, we are dwelling,
In a grand and awful time,
In an age on ages telling
To be living is sublime.
Hark! the waking up of nations,
Gog and Magog to the fray.
Hark! what soundeth is creation
Groaning for its latter day.

Will ye play then, will ye dally
With your music and your wine?
Up! it is Jehovah's rally!
God's own arm hath need of thine.
Hark! the onset! will ye fold your
Faith-clad arms in lazy lock?
Up, oh up, thou drowsy soldier!
Worlds are charging to the shock.

Worlds are charging—heaven beholding;
Thou hast but an hour to fight;
Now the blazoned cross unfolding,
On—right onward for the right.
On! let all the soul within you
For the truth's sake go abroad!
Strike! let every nerve and sinew
Tell on ages—tell for God.

—Arthur Cleveland Coxe

CLEAR THE WAY

MEN of thought! be up and stirring,
    Night and day;
Sow the seed, withdraw the curtain,
    Clear the way!
Men of action, aid and cheer them,
    As ye may!
There's a fount about to stream,
There's a light about to beam,
There's a warmth about to glow,
There's a flower about to blow;
There's midnight blackness changing
    Into gray!
Men of thought and men of action,
    Clear the way!

Once the welcome light has broken,
    Who shall say
What unimagined glories
    Of the day?
What the evil that shall perish
    In its ray?
Aid it, hopes of honest men;
Aid the dawning, tongue and pen;
Aid it, paper, aid it, type,
Aid it, for the hour is ripe;
And our earnest must not slacken
    Into play.
Men of thought and men of action,
    Clear the way!

Lo! a cloud's about to vanish
    From the day;
And a brazen wrong to crumble
    Into clay.
Lo! the Right's about to conquer,
    Clear the way!
With the Right shall many more
Enter, smiling, at the door;
With the giant Wrong shall fall
Many others great and small,
That for ages long have held us
    For their prey.
Men of thought and men of action,
    Clear the way!

—Charles Mackay

WHERE IGNORANCE IS BLISS

T O each his sufferings: all are men,
    Condemned alike to groan;
The tender for another's pain,
    The unfeeling for his own.
Yet, ah! why should they know their fate
Since sorrow never comes too late,
And happiness too swiftly flies?
Thought would destroy their paradise!
No more—where ignorance is bliss
    'Tis folly to be wise.

—Thomas Grey

IN THE HIGHLANDS

I N the highlands, in the country places,
Where the old plain men have rosy faces
And the young fair maidens
    Quiet eyes;
Where essential silence cheers and blesses
And forever in the hill recesses
Her more lovely music
Broods and dies.

Oh, to mount again where erst I haunted,
Where the old red hills are bird enchanted
And the low green meadows
Bright with sward,
And when even dies, the million tinted,
And the night has come and planets glinted,
Lo, the valley hollow,
Lamp bestarred!

Oh, to dream! Oh, to awake and wander
There and with delight to take and render
Through the trance of silence
Quiet breath!
Lo, for there among the flowers and grasses
Only the mightier movement sounds and passes,
Only the winds and rivers
Life and death!

—Robert Louis Stevenson

ON THE PROSPECT OF PLANTING ARTS AND LEARNING IN AMERICA

THE Muse, disgusted at an age and clime
    Barren of every glorious theme,
In distant lands now waits a better time,
    Producing subjects worthy fame.

In happy climes, where from the genial sun
    And virgin earth such scenes ensue,
The force of art by nature seems outdone,
    And fancied beauties by the true.

In happy climes, the seat of innocence,
    Where nature guides and virtue rules,
Where men shall not impose for truth and sense
    The pedantry of courts and schools.

There shall be sung another golden age,
    The rise of empire and of arts,
The good and great inspiring epic rage,
    The wisest heads and noblest hearts.

Not such as Europe breeds in her decay;
    Such as she bred when fresh and young,
When heavenly flame did animate her clay,
    By future poets shall be sung.
    The wisest heads and noblest hearts.

Westward the star of empire takes its way;
    The four first acts already past,
A fifth shall close the drama with the day;
    Time's noblest offspring is the last.

                    —George Bishop Berkeley

WORDS AND ACTS

O put your creed into your deed,
Nor speak with double tongue.

—Emerson

O, CAPTAIN! MY CAPTAIN!

O, Captain! my Captain! our fearful trip is done,
The ship has weather'd every rack, the prize we
      sought is won,
The port is near, the bells I hear, the people all exulting,
While follow eyes the steady keel, the vessel grim and
      daring;
    But, O heart! heart! heart!
      O the bleeding drops of red,
        Where on the deck my Captain lies,
        Fallen cold and dead.

O, Captain! my Captain! rise up and hear the bells;
Rise up—for you the flag is flung—for you the bugle
      trills,
For you bouquets and ribbon'd wreaths—for you the
      shores a-crowding.
For you they call, the swaying mass, their eager faces
      turning;
    Here Captain! dear father!
      This arm beneath your head!
        It is some dream that on the deck,
        You've fallen cold and dead.

My Captain does not answer, his lips are pale and still,
My father does not feel my arm, he has no pulse nor
    will.
The ship is anchor'd safe and sound, its voyage closed
    and done,
From fearful trip the victor ship comes in with object
    won;
    Exult, O shores, and ring, O bells!
      But I with mournful tread
        Walk the deck my Captain lies,
        Fallen cold and dead.

               —Walt Whitman

THE WORLD IS TOO MUCH WITH US

THE world is too much with us; late and soon,
    Getting and spending, we lay waste our powers;
    Little we see in nature that is ours;
We have given our hearts away, a sordid boon!
This sea that bares her bosom to the moon;
    The winds that will be howling at all hours
    And are up-gather'd now like sleeping flowers;
For this, for everything, we are out of tune;
It moves us not. Great God! I'd rather be
    A pagan suckled in a creed outworn;
So I might, standing on this pleasant lea,
    Have glimpses that would make me less forlorn;
Have sight of Proteus rising from the sea,
    Or hear old Triton blow his wreathed horn.

               —William Wordsworth

JUST BE GLAD

OH, heart of mine, we shouldn't
    Worry so!
What we've missed of calm we couldn't
    Have, you know!
What we've met of stormy pain
And of sorrow's driving rain
We can better meet again
    If it blow.

We have erred in that dark hour
    We have known
When our tears fell with the shower,
    All alone—
Were not shine and shower blent
As the gracious Master meant?
Let us temper our content
    With his own.

For, we know, not every morrow
    Can be sad;
So, forgetting all the sorrow
    We have had,
Let us fold away our fears
And put by our foolish tears
And through all the coming years
    Just be glad.

—James Whitcomb Riley

AT THE END OF ALL DESIRE

I AM tired of tears and laughter,
    And men that laugh and weep;
Of what may come hereafter,
    For men that sow to reap:
I am weary of days and hours,
Blown buds of barren flowers,
Desires and dreams and powers,
    And everything but sleep.

We are not sure of sorrow,
    And joy was never sure;
Today will die tomorrow;
    Time stoops to no man's lure;
And love, grown faint and fretful,
With lips but half regretful,
Sighs, and with eyes forgetful,
    Weeps that no loves endure.

From too much love of living,
    From hope and fear set free,
We thank with brief thanksgiving
    Whatever gods may be
That no life lives forever;
That dead men rise up never;
That even the weariest river
    Winds somewhere to the sea.

—Swinburne

JOHN ANDERSON, MY JO

JOHN ANDERSON, my jo, John,
    When we were first acquent,
Your locks were like the raven,
    Your bonnie brow was brent;
But now your brow is beld, John,
    Your locks are like the snaw;
But blessings on your frosty pow
    John Anderson, my jo.

John Anderson, my jo, John,
    We clamb the hill thegither;
And mony a canty day, John,
    We've had wi' ane anither.
Now we maun totter down, John,
    But hand in hand we'll go:
And sleep thegither at the foot,
    John Anderson, my jo.

—Robert Burns

O JOYOUS day! O! Smile of God
    To hearten all who toil and plod;
We hail thee, Conqueror and King!
We hug our golden chains and sing:
    "Good morning!"

—Thomas Augustin Daly

THE SLUGGARD

'TIS the voice of the sluggard; I heard him complain,
"You have wak'd me too soon, I must slumber again."
As the door on its hinges, so he on his bed,
Turns his sides and his shoulders and his heavy head.

"A little more sleep, and a little more slumber,"
Thus he wastes half his days, and his hours without number,
And when he gets up, he sits folding his hands,
Or walks about sauntering, or trifling he stands.

I passed by his garden, and saw the wild brier,
The thorn and the thistle grew broader and higher;
The clothes that hung on him are turning to rags;
And his money still wastes till he starves or he begs.

I made him a visit, still hoping to find
That he took better care for improving his mind;
He told me his dreams, talked of eating and drinking;
But he scarce reads his Bible, and never loves thinking.

Said I then to my heart, "Here's a lesson for me;
This man's but a picture of what I might be;
But thanks to my friends for their care in my breeding,
Who taught me betimes to love working and reading."

—Isaac Watts

FAIR INES

I SAW you not fair Ines?
    She's gone into the West,
To dazzle when the sun is down,
    And rob the world of rest.
She took our daylight with her,
    The smiles that we love best,
With morning blushes on her cheek,
    And pearls upon her breast.

Oh, turn again, fair Ines!
    Before the fall of night,
For fear the moon should shine alone,
    And stars unrivalled bright.
And blessed will the lover be,
    That wakes beneath their light,
And breathes the love against thy cheek,
    I dare not even write!

Would I had been, fair Ines,
    That gallant cavalier,
Who rode so gaily by thy side
    And whispered thee so near!
Were there no loving dames at home,
    Or no true lovers here,
That he should cross the seas to win
    The dearest of the dear?

I saw thee, lovely Ines,
    Descend along the shore,
With a band of noble gentlemen,
    And banners waved before,
And gentle youths and maidens gay—
And snowy plumes they wore;
It would have been a beauteous dream,
—If it had been no more!

Alas, alas, fair Ines!
    She went away with song,
With music waiting on her steps,
    And shouting of the throng.
And some were sad, and felt no mirth,
    But only music's wrong,
In sounds that sang, farewell, farewell!
    To her you've loved so long.

Farewell, farewell, fair Ines,
    That vessel never bore
So fair a lady on its decks,
    Nor danced so light before.
Alas for pleasure on the sea,
    And sorrow on the shore;
The smile that blest one lover's heart,
    Had broken many more!

—Thomas Hood

JUDGE NOT

JUDGE not; the workings of his brain
    And of his heart thou canst not see;
What looks to thy dim eyes a stain,
    In God's pure light may only be
A scar, brought from some well won field,
Where thou wouldst only faint and yield.

The look, the air, that frets thy sight
    May be a token, that below
The soul has closed in deadly fight
    With some infernal fiery foe.
Whose glance would scorch thy smiling grace,
And cast thee shuddering on thy face!

The fall thou darest to despise—
    May be the angel's slackened hand
Has suffered it, that he may rise
    And take a firmer, surer stand;
Or, trusting less to earthly things,
May henceforth learn to use his wings.

And judge none lost; but wait and see,
    With hopeful pity, not disdain;
The depth of the abyss may be
    The measure of the height and pain
And love and glory that may raise
This soul to God in after days!

                        —Adelaide A. Proctor

ABOU BEN ADHEM

ABOU BEN ADHEM (may his tribe increase)!
Awoke one night from a deep dream of peace,
And saw, within the moonlight in his room,
Making it rich, and like a lily in bloom,
An angel writing in a book of gold:
Exceeding peace had made Ben Adhem bold:
And to the presence in the room he said,
"What writest thou?" The vision raised its head,
And with a look made of all sweet accord,
Answered, "The names of those who love the Lord,"
"And is mine one?" said Abou. "Nay, not so."
Replied the angel. Abou spoke more low,
But cheerily still, and said, "I pray thee, then,
Write me as one that loves his fellow-men."

The angel wrote and vanished. The next night
It came again, with a great wakening light,
And showed the names whom love of God had blest,
And, lo! Ben Adhem's name led all the rest.

—Leigh Hunt

HASTE NOT, REST NOT

WITHOUT haste! Without rest!
Bind the motto to thy breast;
Bear it with thee as a spell;
Storm or sunshine, guard it well!
Heed not the flowers that round thee bloom,
Bear it onward to the tomb.

Haste not! Let no thoughtless deed
Mar for aye the spirit's speed!
Ponder well and know the right,
Onward, then, with all thy might!
Haste not! Years can ne'er atone
For one reckless action done.

Rest not! Life is sweeping by,
Go and dare before you die
Something mighty and sublime
Leave behind to conquer time!
Glorious 'tis to live for aye,
When these forms have passed away.

Haste not! Rest not! Calmly wait;
Meekly bear the stones of fate!
Duty be thy polar guide—
Do the right whate'er betide!
Haste not! Rest not! Conflicts past,
God shall crown thy work at last.

—Goethe

PIPPA'S SONG

THE year's at the spring
And day's at the morn;
Morning's at seven;
The hillside's dew-pearled;
The lark's on the wing;
The snail's on the thorn;
God's in his heaven—
All's right with the world.

—Robert Browning

LOVE OF COUNTRY

BREATHES there the man with soul so dead
Who never to himself hath said:
      "This is my own, my native land!"
Whose heart hath ne'er within him burned
As home his footsteps he hath turned,
      From wandering on a foreign strand!
If such there breathe, go mark him well;
For him no minstrel raptures swell;
High though his titles, proud his name,
Boundless his wealth as wish can claim;
Despite those titles, power and pelf,
The wretch concentred all in self,
Living, shall forfeit fair renown,
And, doubly dying, shall go down
To the vile dust from whence he sprung,
Unwept, unhonored, and unsung.

—Sir Walter Scott

COURAGE

WHAT if the morn no joy to you shall bring,
    No gleam of sunbeam shine across your way;
What if no bird one joyous note shall sing
    Into your listening ear through all the day!

What if no word of comfort you shall hear
    As through the hours long you toil and strive;
What if to you no vision bright appear
    To keep your hungry heart and soul alive!

What if the blest companionship men crave
    Come not to you through all the day's long
length,
But, bound and fettered even as a slave,
    Within yourself you have to find your strength!

And if, when you have toiled and wrought alone,
    The sweet reward you sought you do not gain,
And find the hoped-for bread is but stone,
    In that sad hour for grief, should you complain?

Ah no! It matters not if shade or sun,
    Or good or ill, your efforts shall attend;
In doing you have but your duty done
    As best you knew—and should do to the end.

                —Thomas F. Porter

LUCY

 HE dwelt among untrodden ways
    Beside the springs of Dove;
A maid whom there were none to praise
    And very few to love.

A violet by a mossy stone
    Half hidden from the eye—
Fair as a star when only one
    Is shining from the sky.

She lived unknown, and few could know
    When Lucy ceased to be;
But she is in her grave, and O,
    The difference to me!

—William Wordsworth

NOT IN VAIN

F I can stop one heart from breaking,
I shall not live in vain:
If I can ease one life the aching,
Or cool one pain,
Or help one fainting robin
Unto his nest again,
I shall not live in vain.

—Emily Dickinson

PRESS ON

PRESS on! Surmount the rocky steps,
　　Climb boldly o'er the torrent's arch;
He fails alone who feebly creeps,
　　He wins who dares the hero's march.
Be thou a hero! Let thy might
　　Tramp on eternal snows its way,
And through the ebon walls of night
　　Hew down a passage unto day.

Press on! If once and twice thy feet
　　Slip back and stumble, harder try;
From him who never dreads to meet
　　Danger and death they're sure to fly.
To coward ranks the bullet speeds,
　　While on their breasts who never quail,
Gleams, guardian of chivalric deeds,
　　Bright courage like a coat of mail.

Press on! If fortune play thee false
　　Today, tomorrow she'll be true;
Whom now she sinks she now exalts,
　　Taking old gifts and granting new,
The wisdom of the present hour
　　Makes up the follies past and gone;
To weakness strength succeeds, and power
　　From frailty springs! Press on, press on!

　　　　　　　　　　　　—Park Benjamin

FREEDOM

THEY are slaves who fear to speak
For the fallen and the weak;
They are slaves who will not choose
Hatred, scoffing, and abuse,
Rather than in silence shrink
From the truth they needs must think,
They are slaves who dare not be
In the right with two or three.

—James Russell Lowell

SERVICE

WHEN I consider how my light is spent
    Ere half my days, in this dark world and wide,
    And that one talent which is death to hide
Lodged with me useless, though my soul more bent
To serve therewith my Maker, and present
    My true account, lest he returning chide—
    Doth God exact day-labor, light denied?
I fondly ask—but Patience to prevent
That murmur soon-replies: God doth not need
    Either man's work or his own gifts: who best
      Bear his mild yoke, they serve him best:
        His state
Is kingly; thousands at his bidding speed
    And post o'er land and ocean without rest:—
      They also serve who only stand and wait.

—John Milton

HOW TO LIVE

O live, that when thy summons comes to join
The innumerable caravan that moves
To that mysterious realm where each shall take
His chamber in the silent halls of death,
Thou go, not like the quarry slave at night
Scourged to his dungeon, but sustained and soothed
By an unfaltering trust; approach thy grave
Like one who wraps the drapery of his couch
About him, and lies down to pleasant dreams.

—William Cullen Bryant

PROMISE

PPLE orchards, the trees all covered with blossoms;
Wheat fields carpeted far and near in vital emerald
green;
The eternal, exhaustless freshness of each early morning;
The yellow, golden, transparent haze of the warm
afternoon sun;
The aspiring lilac bushes with profuse purple and
white flowers.

—Walt Whitman

CHARACTER OF A HAPPY LIFE

HOW happy is he born and taught
    That serveth not another's will;
Whose armor is his honest thought
    And simple truth his utmost skill!

Whose passions not his masters are,
    Whose soul is still prepared for death,
Not tied unto the world with care
    Of public fame or private breath;

Who envies none that chance doth raise
    Or vice; who never understood
How deepest wounds are given by praise
    Nor rules of state, but rules of good;

Who hath his life from rumors freed,
    Whose conscience is his strong retreat;
Whose state can neither flatterers feed,
    Nor ruin make accusers great;

Who God doth late and early pray
    More of his grace than gifts to lend;
And entertains the harmless day
    With a well-chosen book or friend;

—This man is freed from servile bands
    Of hope to rise or fear to fall;
Lord of himself, though not of lands;
    And having nothing, yet hath all.
                        —Sir H. Wotton

WORTH

HONOR and shame from no condition rise;
Act well your part, there all the honor lies.
Fortune in men has some small diff'rence made,
One flaunts in rags, one flutters in brocade;
The cobbler aproned and the parson gowned,
The friar hooded and the monarch crowned.
"What differ more," you cry, "than crown and cowl?"
I'll tell you, friend: a wise man and a fool.
You'll find, if once the monarch acts the monk,
Or, cobbler-like, the parson will be drunk.
Worth makes the man and want of it the fellow;
The rest is all but leather and prunella.

—Alexander Pope

"HILLS OF HOME"

BLOWS the wind today, and the sun and rain are flying,
Blows the wind on the moors today and now,
Where about the graves of the martyrs the whaups are crying,
My heart remembers how!

Gray, recumbent tombs of the dead in desert places,
Standing stones on the vacant wine-red moor,
Hills of sheep, and the homes of the silent vanished races
And winds, austere and pure.

Be it granted me to behold you again in dying,
Hills of home! and to hear again the call—
Hear about the graves of the martyrs the peewees crying,
And hear no more at all.

—Robert Louis Stevenson

YOUNG AND OLD

HEN all the world is young, lad,
　　When all the trees are green;
And every goose a swan, lad,
　　And every lass a queen;
Then hey for boot and horse, lad,
　　And around the world away;
Young blood must have its course, lad,
　　And every dog his day.

When all the world is old, lad,
　　And all the trees are brown;
And all the sport is stale, lad,
　　And all the wheels run down;
Creep home and take your place there,
　　The spent and maimed among;
God grant you find one face there
　　You loved when all was young.

　　　　　　　　　　—Charles Kingsley

SERENITY

ERE'S a sigh to those who love me
　　And a smile to those who hate;
And whatever sky's above me,
　　Here's a heart for every fate.

　　　　　　　　　　—Lord Byron

Foreword to "Tom Moore"

BE STRONG

E strong,
We are not here to play, to dream, to drift,
We have hard work to do and loads to lift;
Shun not the struggle, face it, 'tis God's gift,
Be strong.

—Maltby D. Babcock

MY CREED

HOLD that Christian grace abounds
    Where charity is seen; that when
We climb to heaven 'tis on the rounds
    Of love to men.

I hold all else named piety
    A selfish scheme, a vain pretense;
Where center is not—can there be
    Circumference ?

This I moreover hold, and dare
    Affirm where'er my rhyme may go—
Whatever things be sweet or fair
    Love makes them so.

Whether it be the lullabies
    That charm to rest the nursling bird,
Or the sweet confidence of sighs
    And blushes, made without a word.

Whether the dazzling and the flush
    Of softly sumptuous garden bowers,
Or by some cabin door a bush
    Of ragged flowers.

'Tis not the wide phylactery,
    Nor stubborn fast, nor stated prayers,
That makes us saints; we judge the tree
    By what it bears.

And when a man can live apart
    From works, on theologic trust,
I know the blood about his heart
    Is dry as dust.

—Alice Cary

HOW SLEEP THE BRAVE

OW sleep the brave who sink to rest
By all their country's wishes blessed!
When Spring, with dewy fingers cold,
Returns to deck their hallowed mold,
She there shall dress a sweeter sod
Than Fancy's feet have ever trod.

By fairy hands their knell is rung,
By forms unseen their dirge is sung;
Their Honor comes, a pilgrim gray,
To bless the turf that wraps their clay;
And Freedom shall awhile repair
To dwell a weeping hermit there.

—William Collins

HOPE

IN the long vista of the years to roll
    Let me not see our country's honor fade!
O let me see our land retain her soul!
    Her pride, her freedom, and not freedom's shade.
From thy bright eyes unusual brightness shed,
Beneath thy pinions canopy my head.

Let me not see the patriot's high bequest,
    Great Liberty! How great in plain attire!
With the base purple of a court oppressed,
    Bowing her head and ready to expire:
But let me see thee stoop from heaven on wings
That fill the sky with silver glitterings.

                                        —John Keats

INVICTUS

OUT of the night that covers me,
    Black as the pit from pole to pole,
I thank whatever gods may be
    For my unconquerable soul.

In the fell clutch of Circumstance
    I have not winced nor cried aloud;
Under the bludgeonings of Chance
    My head is bloody, but unbow'd.

Beyond this place of wrath and tears
    Looms but the horror of the shade,
And yet the menace of the years
    Finds and shall find me unafraid.

It matters not how straight the gate,
    How charged with punishments the scroll,
I am the master of my fate;
    I am the captain of my soul.

           —William Ernest Henley

SERVICE

YET, who, thus looking backward o'er his years,
Feels not his eyelids wet with grateful tears,
    If he hath been
Permitted, weak and sinful as he was,
To cheer and aid in some ennobling cause
    His fellow men ?

If he hath hidden the outcast, or let in
A ray of sunshine to a cell of sin,—
    If he hath lent
Strength to the weak, and, in an hour of need,
Over the suffering, mindless of his creed
    Or home, hath bent,

He hath not lived in vain, and while he gives
The praise to Him, in whom he moves and lives,
　　With thankful heart;
He gazes backward, and with hope before,
Knowing that from his works he nevermore
　　Can henceforth part.

—Whittier

FOR A' THAT

A PRINCE can make a belted knight,
　　A marquis, duke, and a' that;
But an honest man's aboon his might
　　Guid faith he mauna fa' that.
For a' that and a' that,
　　Their dignities and a' that,
The pith o' sense and pride o' worth
　　Are higher ranks than a' that.

Then let us pray that come it may,
　　As come it will for a' that,
That sense and worth, o'er a' the earth,
　　May bear the gree and a' that.
For a' that and a' that,
　　It's coming yet, for a' that,
That man to man, the warld o'er,
　　Shall brothers be for a' that.

—Robert Burns

THE ROSARY OF MY YEARS

SOME reckon their age by years,
    Some measure their life by art,
But some of their days by the flow of their tears,
    And their life by the moans of their heart.
The dials of earth may show
    The length, not the depth of years—
Few or many may come, few or many may go;
    But our time is best measured by tears.
Ah! not by the silver gray
    That creeps through the sunny hair,
And not by the scenes we pass on our way—
    And not by the furrows the finger of Care
In forehead and face has made;
    Not so do we count our years;
Not by the sun of the earth—but by the shade
    Of our souls—and the fall of our tears.
For the young are ofttimes old,
    Though their brow be bright and fair,
While their blood beats warm, their hearts lie cold—
    O'er them the Springtime—but Winter is there,
And the old are ofttimes young,
    When their hair is thin and white;
And they sing in age as in youth they sung,
    And they laugh, for their cross was light.
But bead by bead I tell
    The rosary of my years,
From a cross to a crown they lead—'tis well!
    And they are blessed with a blessing of tears.

Better a day of strife,
    Than a century of sleep;
Give me instead of a long stream of life
    The tempest and tears of the deep.
A thousand joys may foam
    On the billows of all the years;
But never the foam brings the brave bark home—
    It reaches the haven through tears.

—Father Ryan

WHEN IN DISGRACE

WHEN in disgrace with fortune and men's eyes,
I all alone beweep my outcast state,
And trouble deaf Heaven with my bootless cries,
And look upon myself and curse my fate,
Wishing me like to one more rich in hope,
Featured like him, like him with friends possess'd,
Desiring this man's art and that man's scope,
With what I most enjoy contented least;
Yet in these thoughts myself almost despising,
Haply I think on thee—and then my state
(Like to the lark at break of day arising
From sullen earth) sings hymns at heaven's gate;
    For thy sweet love remember'd such wealth brings,
    That then I scorn to change my state with kings.

—Shakespeare

THE SONG OF THE DYING

WE meet 'neath the sounding rafter,
    And the walls around are bare;
As they echo the peals of laughter,
    It seems that the dead are there;
But stand to your glasses steady;
    We drink to our comrades' eyes,
Quaff a cup to the dead already—
    And hurrah for the next that dies!

Time was when we frowned at others;
    We thought we were wiser then;
Ha! Ha! Let those think of mothers
    Who hope to see them again.
No! Stand to your glasses steady;
    The thoughtless are here the wise;
A cup to the dead already—
    Hurrah for the next that dies!

There's many a hand that's shaking,
    There's many a cheek that's sunk;
But soon, tho' our hearts are breaking,
    They'll burn with the wine we have drunk.
So stand to your glasses steady—
    'Tis here the revival lies;
A cup to the dead already—
    And hurrah for the next that dies!

Who dreads to the dust returning?
　　Who shrinks from the sable shore,
Where the high and haughty yearning
　　Of the soul shall sting no more?
Ho! stand to your glasses steady—
　　This world is a world of lies;
A cup for the dead already—
　　Hurrah for the next that dies!

Cut off from the land that bore us,
　　Betrayed by the land we find,
Where the brightest have gone before us,
　　And the dullest remain behind—
Stand, stand to your glasses steady,
　　'Tis all we have left to prize;
A cup to the dead already—
　　And hurrah for the next that dies!

PERSEVERANCE

WE must not hope to be mowers,
　　And to gather the ripe gold ears,
Unless we have first been sowers
　　And watered the furrows with tears.

It is not just as we take it,
　　This mystical world of ours,
Life's field will yield as we make it
　　A harvest of thorns or of flowers.

—Goethe

IT'S RAINING VIOLETS

 T is not raining rain to me,
    It's raining daffodils;
In every dimpled drop I see
    Wild flowers on the hills.

The clouds of gray engulf the day,
    And overwhelm the town;
It is not raining rain to me,
    It's raining roses down.

It is not raining rain to me,
    But fields of clover bloom,
Where any buccaneering bee
    May find a bed and room.

A health unto the happy!
    A fig for him who frets;
It is not raining rain to me,
    It's raining violets.

            —Robert Loveman

THE ISLE OF LONG AGO

OH, a wonderful stream is the River Time,
    As it flows through the realm of years,
With a faultless rhythm and a musical rhyme,
And a broader sweep and a surge sublime,
    As it blends with the ocean of years.

How the winters are drifting, like flakes of snow,
    And the summers like buds between;
And the years in the sheaf—so they come and they go
On the river's breast, with its ebb and flow,
    As they glide in the shadow and sheen.

There's a magical Isle up the River Time,
    Where the softest of airs are playing,
There's a cloudless sky and a tropical clime,
And a voice as sweet as a vesper chime,
    And the Junes with the roses are staying.

And the name of this Isle is the Long Ago,
    And we bury our treasures there;
There are brows of beauty and bosoms of snow—
There are heaps of dust, but we love them so!
    There are trinkets and tresses of hair.

There are fragments of songs that nobody sings,
    And a part of an infant's prayer,
There's a harp unswept and a lute without strings,
There are broken vows and pieces of rings,
    And the garments she used to wear.

There are hands that are waved when the fairy shore
    By the mirage is lifted in air;
And we sometimes hear through the turbulent roar
Sweet voices we heard in the days gone before,
    When the wind down the river is fair.

Oh, remembered for aye be the blessed Isle
    All the day of our life till night,
And when evening comes with its beautiful smile,
And our eyes are closing in slumber awhile,
May that "Greenwood" of soul be in sight.

           —Benjamin F. Taylor

THE SPLENDOR FALLS

THE splendor falls on castle walls
    And snowy summits old in story;
The long light shakes across the lakes
    And the wild cataract leaps in glory,
Blow, bugle, blow, set the wild echoes flying,
Blow, bugle; answer, echoes, dying, dying, dying.

O hark! O hear! how thin and clear,
    And thinner, clearer, farther going!
O sweet and far from cliff and scar
    The horns of Elfland faintly blowing!
Blow, let us hear the purple glens replying;
Blow, bugle; answer, echoes, dying, dying, dying.

O love, they die in yon rich sky,
    They faint on hill or field or river;
Our echoes roll from soul to soul,
    And grow forever and forever,
Blow, bugle, blow, set the wild echoes flying,
And answer, echoes, answer, dying, dying, dying.

                            —Alfred Tennyson

CROSSING THE BAR

UNSET and evening star,
    And one clear call for me,
And may there be no moaning of the bar,
    When I put out to sea.

But such a tide as moving seems asleep,
    Too full for sound and foam,
When that which drew from out the boundless deep,
    Turns again home.

Twilight and evening bell,
    And after that the dark;
And may there be no sadness of farewell,
    When I embark.

For tho' from out our bourne of time and place,
    The flood may bear me far,
I hope to see my Pilot face to face
    When I have crossed the bar.

                            —Tennyson

THE WORLD OVER

IN vain we call old notions fudge,
    And bend our conscience to our dealing;
The Ten Commandments will not budge,
    And stealing will continue stealing.

—Lowell

A PSALM OF LIFE

TELL me not in mournful numbers
    Life is but an empty dream,
For the soul is dead that slumbers,
    And things are not what they seem.

Life is real! Life is earnest!
    And the grave is not its goal;
Dust thou art, to dust returnest,
    Was not spoken of the soul.

Not enjoyment, and not sorrow,
    Is our destined end or way;
But to act, that each tomorrow
    Find us farther than today.

Art is long and Time is fleeting,
    And our hearts, though stout and brave,
Still, like muffled drums, are beating
    Funeral marches to the grave.

In the world's broad field of battle,
    In the bivouac of Life,
Be not like dumb, driven cattle!
    Be a hero in the strife!

Trust no future, howe'er pleasant!
    Let the dead Past bury its dead!
Act—act in the living present!
    Heart within and God o'erhead.

Lives of great men all remind us
    We can make our lives sublime,
And, departing, leave behind us
    Footprints on the sands of time.

Footprints, that perhaps another,
    Sailing o'er life's solemn main,
A forlorn and shipwrecked brother,
    Seeing, shall take heart again.

Let us, then, be up and doing,
    With a heart for any fate;
Still achieving, still pursuing,
    Learn to labor and to wait.

—H. W. Longfellow

THE SPRING OF LOVE

A LITTLE sun, a little rain,
    O soft wind blowing from the West,
And woods and fields are sweet again
    And Warmth within the mountain's breast.

A little love, a little trust,
    A soft impulse, a sudden dream,
And life as dry as desert dust,
    Is fresher than a mountain stream.

—Stopford A. Brooks

UNSUBDUED

I HAVE hoped, I have planned, I have striven,
    To the will I have added the deed;
The best that was in me I've given,
    I have prayed, but the gods would not heed.

I have dared and reached only disaster,
    I have battled and broken my lance;
I am bruised by a pitiless master
    That the weak and the timid call chance.

I am old, I am bent, I am cheated
    Of all that Youth urged me to win;
But name me not with the defeated,
    Tomorrow again, I begin.

—S. E. Kiser

SYMPATHY

'Tis a little thing
O give a cup of water; yet its draught
Of cool refreshment, drained by fevered lips,
May give a shock of pleasure to the frame
More exquisite than when nectarean juice
Renews the life of joy in happier hours.
It is a little thing to speak a phrase
Of common comfort which by daily use
Has almost lost its sense, yet on the ear
Of him who thought to die unmourned 'twill fall
Like choicest music, fill the glazing eye
With gentle tears, relax the knotted hand
To know the bonds of fellowship again;
And shed on the departing soul a sense,
More precious than the benison of friends
About the honored deathbed of the rich,
To him who else were lonely, that another
Of the great family is near and feels.

—Sir Thomas N. Talfourd

BELIEVE not each accusing tongue,
    As most weak persons do;
But still believe that story wrong
    Which ought not be true.

—Sheridan

TWO things there are with Memory will abide,
    Whatever else befall, while life flows by;
That soft, cold hand-touch at the altar side;
    The thrill that shook you at your child's first cry.

                                —Thomas Bailey Aldrich

LEAD KINDLY LIGHT

LEAD, kindly Light, amid the encircling gloom,
    Lead thou me on!
The night is dark and I am far from home,
    Lead thou me on!
Keep thou my feet; I do not ask to see
The distant scene—one step enough for me.

I was not ever thus, nor prayed that thou
    Shouldst lead me on;
I loved to see and choose my path, but now
    Lead thou me on!
I loved the garish day, and, spite of fears,
Pride ruled my will: remember not past years.

So long thy power hath blessed me, sure it still
    Will lead me on;
O'er moor and fen, o'er crag and torrent till
    The night is gone;
And with the morn those angel faces smile
Which I have loved long since, and lost awhile.

                                —John Henry (Cardinal) Newman

PASS UNDER THE ROD

SAW the young bride in her beauty and pride,
    Bedecked in her snowy array;
And the bright flush of joy mantled high on her cheek
    And the future looked blooming and gay;
And with woman's devotion she laid her fond heart
    At the shrine of idolatrous love;
And she anchored her hopes to this perishing earth,
    By the chain which her tenderness wove.
But I saw when those heart-strings were bleeding and torn,
    And the chain had been severed in two;
She had changed her white robes for sables of grief,
    And her bloom for the paleness of woe!
But the Healer was there, pouring balm on her heart,
    And wiping the tears from her eyes;
He strengthened the chain He had broken in twain,
    And fastened it firm to the skies!
There had whispered a voice—'twas the voice of her God:
"I love thee! I love thee! Pass under the rod!"

I saw a young mother in tenderness bend
    O'er the couch of her slumbering boy;
And she kissed the soft lips as they murmured her name,
    While the dreamer lay smiling in joy.
O, sweet as the rosebud encircled with dew,
    When its fragrance is flung in the air,
So fresh and so bright to that mother he seemed,
    As he lay in his innocence there.
But I saw when she gazed on the same lovely form,

Pale as marble and silent and cold;
But paler and colder her beautiful boy,
    And the tale of her sorrow was told.
But the Healer was there who had stricken her heart
    And taken her treasure away;
To allure her to heaven He has placed it on high,
    And the mourner will sweetly obey:
There had whispered a voice—'twas the voice of her God:
"I love thee! I love thee! Pass under the rod!"

I saw a fond father and mother who leaned
    On the arms of a dear, gifted son;
And the star in the future grew bright to their gaze,
    As they saw the proud place he had won;
And the fast-coming evening of life promised fair,
    And its pathway grew smooth to their feet
And the starlight of love glimmered bright at his end,
    And the whispers of fancy were sweet.
And I saw them again bending low o'er his grave,
    Where their hearts' clearest hopes had been laid;
And the star had gone down in the darkness of night,
    And the joy from their bosoms had fled.
But the Healer was there, and His arms were around,
    And he led them with tenderer care;
And He showed them a star in the bright upper world,
    'Twas their star shining brilliantly there!
They had each heard a voice—'twas the voice of their God:
"I love thee! I love thee! Pass under the rod!"

—Mrs. M. S. B. Dana

THE CHAMBERED NAUTILUS

THIS is the ship of pearl, which, poets feign,
    Sails the unshadowed main—
    The venturous bark that flings
On the sweet Summer wind its purpled wings
In gulfs enchanted, where the siren sings,
    And coral reefs lie bare,
Where the cold sea-maids rise to sun their streaming hair.

Its webs of living gauze no more unfurl;
    Wrecked is the ship of pearl!
    And every chambered cell,
Where its dim dreaming life was wont to dwell,
And the frail tenant shaped his growing shell,
    Before thee lies revealed—
Its iris ceiling rent, its sunless crypt unsealed!

Year after year beheld the silent toil
    That spread his lustrous coil;
    Still, as the spiral grew,
He left the past year's dwelling for the new,
Stole with soft step its shining archway through,
    Built up its idle door,
Stretched in his last-found home, and knew the old no more.

Thanks for the heavenly message brought by thee,
    Child of the wandering sea,
    Cast from her lap forlorn!
From thy dead lips a clearer note is born
Than ever Triton blew from wreathed horn!
    While on mine ear it rings,
Through the deep caves of thought I hear a voice that sings:—

Build thee more stately mansions, O my soul,
    As the swift seasons roll!
    Leave thy low-vaulted past!
Let each new temple, nobler than the last,
Shut thee from heaven with a dome more vast,
    Till thou at length art free,
Leaving thine outgrown shell by life's unresting sea.

                —Oliver Wendell Holmes

BALANCING

THE good we meant to do—the deeds
    So oft misunderstood;
The thwarted good we try to do,
    And would do, if we could,
The noble deeds we set upon
    And have accomplished none—
Write them—and with them credit all
    The bad we have not done.

              —Wilbur D. Nesbit

L'ENVOI

WHEN earth's last picture is painted, and the tubes
    are twisted and dried,
When the oldest colors have faded, and the youngest
    critic has died.
We shall rest, and, faith, we shall need it—lie down for
    an aeon or two.
Till the Master of All Good Workmen shall set us to
    work anew!

And those that were good will be happy: they shall sit
    in a golden chair;
They shall splash at a ten-league canvas with brushes
    of comet's hair;
They shall find real saints to draw from—Magdalene,
    Peter and Paul;
They shall work for an age at a sitting and never be
    tired at all;

And only the Master shall praise us, and only the
    Master shall blame;
And no one shall work for money, and no one shall
    work for fame;
But each for the joy of the working, and each, in his
    separate star,
Shall draw the Thing as he sees It for the God of
    Things as They Are!

—Rudyard Kipling